The narrative essays that comprise "Coriander" defy categorization, reflecting the complex theme of identity that runs throughout the book. What does it mean to be a daughter, a mother, a professional, a friend, a lover, a woman defining who she is against the backdrop of external definitions in a world where labels of gender, race, and ethnicity are inescapable? The writing is unforgettably lyrical, humorous, heart-wrenching, instructive, engaging, and always fully human. The strength of this collection is that it reaches beyond memoir in providing a glimpse of the author's internal journey and lived experiences, as it invites the reader to self-reflect on similar questions of meaning and identity.

Dr. Michelle Porche,
Associate Director and Senior Research Scientist,
Wellesley Centers for Women, Wellesley College.

Coriander:

A Collection of Narrative Essays

By
Gia Bernini

For Juliet and Gabriel, my forever blessing.

Contents

Mine and Them

What Happens
When You Leave Me

Belief and Relief: Thank you God

Acknowledgments

I would like to thank Linda McCullough Moore, a mentor and endless encourager who has a hawk's eye for finding the best in one's writing.

I would like to thank my family members, Ema, Daniel, and Gloria, who nodded their heads in approval when I read my work to them, and told me to keep on writing.

I would like to thank Danny, the hardest-working artist I know, for his early encouragement.

I would like to thank Lila, Lillian, Luz Eneida, Emma, Nancy, Alice, Lourdes, Dee, Sarah, Rachel, Aimee, Miguel, Pedro and the Ecuadorian community of Western Massachusetts for sharing time, thoughts and observations on life that inspired me to write.

I would like to thank the following kindred spirits who brought their own skill, craft and creativity to support the manifestation of this book: Libby Maxey, Johanna Renard, Alison Hornbeck, Rosie McMahan, Romana Lowe, Lisa Fortuna, Michelle Porche, Levellers Press, Caleb Wetmore, Steve Strimer, and Faith Seddon.

I would like to thank the participants of Linda McCullough Moore writer's workshop for creating an especially loving space for writing.

Finally, I am forever grateful to Manuel and his family for opening the doors and windows within me to a culture and faith.

Chapter I

The Melting Pot

Gravel

I am awaiting two truckloads of forty tons of gravel, the kind used to make a dirt driveway. I already have a dirt driveway, or what is left of an old asphalt driveway, but I want to renew it with fresh gravel with more consistency, not a mixture of broken asphalt and natural rock that erupts from the ground with each tire spin. I'm following the instinct of an ant, moving sand and earth from here to there, always fixing the place where I live. I'm following deep patterns, and who can blame me? What else do we do on Earth but keep ourselves busy moving piles of things from one side of the planet to the other?

But what does that driveway mean to me? What will the dark grey gravel path lined with bordering bricks signify to my fellow human beings? Will I rise in esteem? Will I receive the gentle hand waves, nods, and side-glances of approval from my neighbors as they drive by the new driveway? Maybe Henry will tell Hannah, "They finally got the driveway redone. About time! The street was turning into a dump. I remember when Mr. Colt owned that house, how he kept up his yard, not a dry leaf on the lawn!"

I want to slide onto a new spot on the checkerboard of social standing. No longer will my driveway be chosen for the destructive three-point turns of lost travelers and browsing visitors on tag sale day. We'll be the nice little couple who "really did something to that house."

And why do I care what they think? Deeper patterns. Deep fissures. I want to belong. This is the motive underneath my forty tons of gravel. I want to scuttle back into my home like a crab into its shell and look out upon accepting faces. Instead I've let the years accumulate in one place, and still, when I turn around, I don't feel the soft inner contours of the homey shell. The building is there. The home is not. The neighbors are there. Their approving nods are not.

The concept of *home* seems to belong to other people, but not to me. I spend time with immigrants who have a home elsewhere. They ask me, "Is this your house or do your rent it?" and I say, "I own it," although I look at the house as if it belongs to someone else. These same immigrants tell me I'm an American, and I smile kindly, but the term doesn't resonate within me. I am an empty shell. What is it to be American? Is it to own a home in the United States and owe a lifetime of money to a bank called Bank of America? Is it to have been born within these fifty states? Is it to want your Anglo neighbors to approve of your new driveway?

I am still waiting for the forty tons of gravel. The front loader will come tear up what is left of the old asphalt. We will dig deeper. I hope the forty tons will be enough to cover all the holes and dips of the old driveway. I hope it will bury all of the doubt and insecurity of a life caught in between cultures. I hope it will anchor my feet and spirit to the ground of a place called home.

Flea Market

We scan the flea market under the autumnal New England sun for military clothing. We find the green and brown patterned uniform with a partially-ripped name patch on the chest. I try to pronounce the Italian surname, and you say you'll just rip off the patch. I wonder about the young man who completed enough tours in Iraq or Afghanistan to pack that duffle bag one last time and get rid of it all.

"Maybe this belongs to a dead soldier!" I warn you, picturing a tearful aunt dropping off the duffle bag at the Goodwill.

You smile at me under the brilliant blue sky.

"Everything can be recycled."

Bending over to rummage through the box of clothes, you add, "The farm workers love these. They are good for working in the fields. It gets cold in the mountains."

I remember our mission to collect clothing for your mother to sell on her trips to coffee plantations in Nicaragua. She told me that the farm workers would buy anything. They had cash in hand, and preferred to buy on the plantation rather than pay to travel to a neighboring town.

A little over twenty years ago, my parents met eagerly with serious friends and discussed moving to Nicaragua to support the Sandinista revolution. Somehow they didn't go. Maybe their marriage was not stable or they couldn't uproot me. I was an adolescent trying to squeeze myself into too-tight jeans, and I wanted to remain loyal to the secret society of American youth. But the horror of the Contra's tactics against the Nicaraguan people was well documented in my home. My father would stand in our small kitchen and explain to all present that the School of the Americas was producing killers and instructing them to set mines to blow off arms and legs, leaving survivors to drag their dream of a socialist, egalitarian society into the mud. Those years were peppered with stories of terrible massacres throughout Central America; women raped here, people decapitated there, and indigenous villages digging their own mass graves further over there. I could live my happy life in the States, but I would not be spared the knowledge that my standard of living was built on the exploitation and violation of human rights elsewhere.

Now, I lie with you and watch your chest rise in the morning light, son of a Sandinista who died when you were just three. Your father, a kaleidoscope of stories others have told you, a man who enforced Sandinista law in the small community spreading up the mountainside beyond the city nestled in the valley. Crazed by the war, he collected weaponry. Your mother, just a girl when he took her, recounts him shooting at her feet when he was angry. A hero, he saved his nephew from death and threw him off the motorbike before careening into the bus that took his life.

You look like him, they say. You like guns, too. An immigrant here, you've been sent with one mission: to make money for your family back home. There is no war, only a black and red Sandinista flag and no work to be had in Nicaragua. Your hands are dry with cement powder and there is sand in your hair. There is no enemy to fight here, only the silence of a language you don't understand.

We make trips to the flea market. You want to see familiar faces and talk a little. We eat rice and fried chicken at the Chinese lady's booth. You shake hands with the Puerto Rican guy who sells stolen goods. "Brother, how are you?" you ask him. I smile and nod. I'm with you.

But who am I? Who are we? We belong here at the flea market. We rifle through bins looking for military clothes to recycle. We are what has been left after the war, after the revolutionary movements, those who have lived with and without, but maybe of value to someone, somewhere.

Who are you?

Who are you?

I am the product of some poor, white, Wal-Mart G-string wearing, dyed-almost-blonde woman with a pocketbook filled with scratch tickets and menthol lights and a tall Puerto Rican who ducks when he enters a room, doesn't say much, and magically knows something about fixing cars, but otherwise has never been seen, only sensed on the other end of the cell phone call.

I am the brainchild of two lesbians who planned and discussed and emailed each other, *"I know you are at work, but please look at the two donor candidates I sent you attached, Hon, … This is what I was talking about last night"* and invested in making a child with a multicultural dimension because one of them had ancestors from somewhere.

I am the daughter of a white, American woman who studied Spanish in college because she had hopes of working internationally, but instead found herself drunk, high, and kneeling in front of his truck as he injected her with the genetic blend of a short, indigenous, barefoot Indian and a sweaty, chauvinist, Spanish conquistador.

I am the baby they "made in America" the first night when she was delivered by van to New York after driving twenty hours straight from Texas, desert sand still in her hair and their golden crowned teeth flashing in the night as they curled up on the mattress on the floor.

I am the child made by a teenage mother in foster care, who can't say who the father is and sits with the flat face of a concussed patient, too many smacks to the head at the age of two, peeling her nail polish off with her teeth.

I am the adopted child of a Christian couple who had strong values and wanted to "do good in the world," but whose benevolence melted like the ice in the cocktail glass she clung onto when her missionary hubby had his second affair.

I am not the child of a Latina who shivered by her blue-eyed husband's side in the New England cold and stood waiting on the wooden porch of that Victorian house to be welcomed in by her in-laws, and is still waiting.

I am that child, I am that child and yet I am not.

Multi

Multi-cultural, tri-lingual, bi-cultural, bi-racial. Would that these words bring an experience of wholeness to the person who embodies them. But they do not for me. Speaking more than one language, knowing more than one culture, and growing up in more than one country has meant, for me, a suspended existence. I am forever the outsider. Strangely enough, even years spent living in one place has not removed from me the feeling that I am an outsider. I may know the language, dress like everyone else, have the title at the end of my name, own the house and the car, yet I am still a visitor. An illegitimate fog seeps into me when I least expect it.

I tell myself that I am part of the majority now. Even the president of this "great nation" has, like me, lived in a mix of cultures. And yet I can't step out of the role of observer. I am a witness to others who seem to move through their lives like fish in water—so confident inside their environment.

In the United States being Latina or Spanish-speaking is perceived by my English-speaking compatriots as something that I *have*. They have told me how they wish to have that cultural trait, that ethnicity. Like the scarf a supervisor gave me as a farewell present when I was leaving a job.

"I picked this scarf for you, because it's ethnic, and you're so ethnic," she said, her hand gesturing in my direction.

I smiled and thanked her. It was a beautiful multicolored scarf and I wore it. I have been called ethnic before.

I wonder now if the supervisor remembers me, her ethnic assistant. I certainly remember her and how she invited me to her birthday party at a university college hall, where she performed a tap dance for her guests. She was blond and turning sixty. She put on a black leotard and the party guests made a circle to give her room to dance. We tried not to drop the food from our paper plates on each other as she tapped by thrusting herself so confidently forward and back.

When I am in my country of ethnic origin, Colombia, I might as well be standing naked with only the American flag to cover me. I understand the language and the culture enough to know that I can never be entirely part of it. I'm slow to catch fleeting humor, I don't have any sayings at my disposal, I don't know the names of fruit or vegetables, and I stand too tall. Worse, I want to be alone sometimes. In any Latin country, I'm always an American and still I yearn to be one of them.

Back home, the vague feeling of inauthenticity also exists. My childhood was characterized by many moves from one country to another. As an adult, I wanted to put down roots. My own desire for stability and attachment to one culture led me to raise my children in an American, English-speaking, middle-class environment. They look upon my Latino ethnicity and the Spanish language as a familiar quirk, like a strangely shaped earlobe or a cowlick that requires careful hairdressing. I can't help but repeat and remind them that they, too, are Latinos. Now in their adolescent years, my children curl their lips in a slight discomfort when anything associated with Latino culture is offered. I know this is normal for teenagers. Still, this mild rejection hurts me, beyond the tug of their average individuation. I remind them that one day when they are looking for scholarship money to attend a predominately white university, they are going to want to check off the box next to *Latino*. They look at me confused, and I am confused as well. How much Latino do you need to be Latino? The definition of ethnicity and race, the authenticity that comes with these social constructs, is beyond me.

All I am left with is that ungrounded feeling, like a red balloon lifting off untethered, pushed by the air currents and alone. I know I have something special, but it is elusive and seems to take away power and then give power back depending on the circumstances.

How many times have I been told, "Oh, thank God you can speak Spanish!" and asked, "Can you translate to them what I'm saying?" or, "Oh, your English is so good, you don't have an accent!" Too many times!

I can't escape this reality. I am stuck on the fence. I might have a better view but I am too high and sometimes teetering.

Immigration Dream

It's two in the afternoon. Piles of papers are re-producing and populating the bed. I look over the worried, worn discharge papers, re-reading the date and inspecting the fine print. They reflect back:

"Alien number, A1234567 Detainee Name: Jose, Alvarez, Velasquez, Torres."

These are the names of hairy conquistadores with heated loins. And here over the typed name, an immigration judge has scrawled his signature like an indifferent doctor. Is it really Smith or Jones, or better yet, a good Irish name, like McCarthy, McNamara, or Finn? I can smell the acrid beer that the judge drank over lunch in the back booth at a local restaurant. It is a step up from a diner but has the same artery-inflaming menu. I know I saw him there.

The judge sits in judgment in a newly built facility at the end of an industrial road called Federal Drive, or State Drive, or Constitution Drive, somewhere in the United States off a state highway, with tolls, and blue and beige cars waiting at every hill, scanners at the ready. "License and registration, please." That is how Jose, descendant of a Spanish conquistador,

African slaves, and Indigenous people, got an Alien number.

I study the photocopied resources given to persons awaiting deportation proceedings. I am squinting now, trying to understand what qualifies as a defense to prevent deportation. I can't understand. I wonder, is this really such a wonderful country? I heard them say on the radio that this economy was going down the tubes along with European countries like Greece and Portugal that I once dreamed of visiting. And what about the environment? Could my little garden that froze to a deathly brown color over the winter support my family's appetite? I think there is a better chance of eating all year long in warmer climates. Maybe we will be lining up at the doors of Central American embassies soon enough, documents in hand with new terms like "environmental refugees."

In the meantime, waves of immigrants, survivors of nightmares, cross over the Mexican border, their eyes wide and their bodies reverberating with the violence they experienced. Deportation is the ever-present hand of the law weighing on the immigrant's chest. It is a monster with many faces. Immigrants want to work and make money, stay alive, and keep their families back home alive as well. It is really that simple. But it isn't. Only an immigration lawyer can file the right paperwork. Only an immigration lawyer who will charge a hundred and fifty dollars for a half an hour consult, and another who will charge five thousand can keep you from being deported in six months. Time to go mow lawns and rake leaves for eight dollars an hour. *¡A trabajar!*

On TV, I watch an interview with a border guard. A blue-eyed man, his waist weighed down with black weaponry, says, "I put my life on the line every day for my country." That is what he thinks before he begins the game of cat and mouse, in the dry lands of the South. *What country is he talking about?* I ask myself. Does the eagle gliding on the warm air currents see the difference between one country and another?

I am the daughter of immigrants, British immigrants who arrived three hundred years ago on one side and South American immigrants who arrived less than fifty years ago on the other. I happen to look like those crawling on their bellies in the Arizona sand, but I also look like the Italians who filled the north and south ends of cities at the turn of the century. And yet I am of no blood relation. I just happened to walk tall and speak without an accent because my mother gave birth to me into the hands of a North American doctor whom she could not understand. He welcomed me into American life with a good, hard slap on my bottom. I believe I've had mixed feelings about being American ever since.

I look back down at the deportation papers and the Alien number before me. I have a few numbers attached to my name, too: a social security number and a United States passport number. In this version of the American dream, they are lucky numbers, as were the alignment of stars in the North American sky, the winter night I was born on this side of the border.

Backyard American Dream

I see the speckled black and white bantam chicken moving with her three adopted turkey chicks outside the backyard and beyond my fence, pecking at fresh new ground. The fence was supposed to be fixed so no chickens could pass. It was the job of the men I live with, two brothers, short, dark skinned Nicaraguan men, who insist on letting all animals loose in the backyard, including two rabbits, who came with a lovely rabbit hutch and water bottle at their disposal. I used to bring the rabbits treats of hand-cut grass and kitchen scraps. One of the brothers says, "Now they can get all the treats they want for themselves." He is the one who promised he would be able to catch the rabbits after he gave them the chance to be free and run around. Now the rabbits lie on the grass in the shade. It seems bucolic enough. He reports proudly, his hands on his hips, tipping his Yankee baseball cap, that they are breeding with each other and that the female has a nest in the shed. He apparently thinks that is the point of every life form, to reproduce itself. Sometimes I wish these men didn't live with me.

I want to be normal like the neighbor across the street. He's got a dog. He also spent a boatload of money on a fence for his Newfoundland. The six-month-old puppy is walked up and down the street every day, stopping at the end of his leash to be loved by all the neighbors. "Wow, he is getting big!" they say. "Yes, you're a cute baby!" they tell the dog. "I saw you put up a beautiful fence. It looks good," they tell my normal neighbor.

Meanwhile back at the ranch, there is a red Mustang in my backyard that is serving as shade for chickens. The Mustang belongs to one of the brothers. It is the first car that he purchased in the United States. He doesn't drive his American dream car because in its current form it's a magnet for speeding tickets and it almost put an end to the American dream. I didn't want the car to be parked there initially. I tried to tell him it makes me look like white trash. But there isn't a word for that in Spanish, and there probably shouldn't be one in English either. So I told him I don't want to be the type of person who has an abandoned car in my backyard. He answered smiling, "It's not abandoned! I love this car. It just needs to be painted a different color."

I must admit sometimes I don't even notice the car, except when we watch the chicks hopping up into what I believe is the engine. I guess that is what happens. You get used to it being there, the bright dream, the hope, the future, and then it begins to rot into the landscape and you don't see it anymore.

A home says everything about a person. My home says that I am a mixed breed, which I am. My great-grandmother's baby Steinway that sits like a huge paperweight in my front living room doesn't really belong in a ranch. It fits better in my grandmother's Victorian living room, near the greenhouse, and the smell of forced winter tulip bulbs. I have a brightly decorated kitchen, drawing on colors of places where I would rather live, like France, Italy, and Spain. Places where I would always be the American, the foreigner, where people would invite me to their homes to try regional dishes, and like a mascot I would be paraded around town. And even if I stayed and was permitted an extended visa, I would still be called the American, no matter how well I learned the dialect, or the butcher knew my favorite cuts of meat.

But here, in the country and state where I was born, I am too mixed. I am too many broken pieces to be put together. Being normal is as elusive to me as those two rabbits lying in the shade. I lunge to try to catch one to put it back into the rabbit hutch, and it hops just out of my grasp. "Come and try to get me!" the rabbit winks. Some days I just want to get rid of them.

Things keep sticking out wherever I live; there are the dark skinned brothers who sing out Rancheras into the dark night sky, and a red Mustang that sits like a large mushroom in the backyard. There are winking rabbits that hop into the air with the joy they feel. And the chicken with her adopted turkey chicks slip through the holes in the fence, and walk proudly across the front yard for all to see, their feathers shining under the sun.

Night of the Living Bible

It's a cool night and the sun is setting earlier and earlier so I drive home in twilight. There at the end of the driveway, I see the light of the one bulb in the garage shining out through the steamed windows. Inside the garage, my Ecuadorean neighbors are butchering a lamb. I come in the side door and smell the warm odor of sheep wool and blood. The two women turn and smile cautiously.

"Hello, hello," I say.

"Hello," they answer.

"I came too late!" I say. The animal has already been divided up into portions and placed in white buckets, and they are picking up the cleaver and knives from the shiny dark green tarp.

"You are his wife?" one woman asks. Loose strands of her long, dark ponytail hang down the side of her Andean face. She wipes them away with her forearm and points to my partner who is untying the rigging.

"Yes," I say. After all, who would want to explain how it's complicated over steaming lamb shanks?

Her own husband speaks up, "It is so kind of you to let us do this here. I hope you will join us Saturday for the feast! We are so blessed. We will be singing in Quechua but ...." He doesn't finish.

His eyes are dark and glassy. We've talked before. He is an Evangelical Christian. When he feels blessed and the Holy Spirit fills his chest, the feeling hardly lets him speak.

His wife adds, "We will be singing in Spanish, too. I hope you are coming."

I say, "Yes, we will be there! Of course!"

I move toward the cleaver, small axe, and knife. "Are these ready to be washed?"

I know the only way to make people feel welcome is to join in and begin helping.

"Yes," the other woman says. She is picking up four hooves and dropping them into another white bucket.

I can't resist. "Will you use those too?" I ask.

"Yes," she says, one hoof in hand, "we take off the wool—" she demonstrates with her small skillful fingers pulling on the grey fur "—and use it, too, and it makes good soup!"

I smile. "It's going to be wonderful," I say.

The Christian man has regained his voice and says, "We use everything. We don't waste a thing." The light shines on proud faces and reflects off the tan and dark parts that sit steaming in the buckets.

We go back to our chores. In fifteen minutes, the garage is empty. The green tarp is washed and folded and the garage floor smells of citrus cleaning solution. We stand in the middle, hands on our hips, nodding while the Christian man repeats how blessed we are, and thanks God for people like us who help their fellow man. I remember that it's time to pick up my daughter from her soccer game. I politely retire from the group, jump into the car, and drive through the night to the illuminated field.

Under the floodlights, the varsity soccer team is running up the field. My daughter is in the stands, tucked in next to her own junior varsity teammates to keep warm. She is expected to watch the first half of the varsity game and does so religiously. I go stand by the chain-link fence looking to get her attention. I text, call, and wave to her, but she doesn't see me. She is with her own, girls with blue, white, and yellow uniforms and brown, black, and blond ponytails. They are laughing and shoving each other. Finally, a slow moving triad of girls walks by, and I call out to them through the fence.

"Can you get Juliet's attention for me?" I ask the girls. With little frowns of discomfort, they agree to fetch her for me. My daughter jumps down the bleacher stairs, her ponytail swishing back and forth. She is my own happy lamb, leaving the flock to join me.

"Sorry Mom, I don't have my cell phone. I left it at Sarah's."

We drive home, and she leans over to put on the hip-hop radio station. I won't tell her about the sheep butchered in the garage or about the Ecuadorean Christians. It is too far away a world for her to imagine. Still, I feel like my chest is bursting with joy because they both exist. So I say out to the darkness, "God, thank you for blessing us this night."

Chapter II

Oh So Human!

A Hospital Stay

She appeared in the doorway, hair disheveled and held back from her pale face by a thick purple headband.

"I was in this room before," she said, pointing at us.

"I was here for two weeks, and they put me in this room. You can see everything that is happening from this room; you can see right down the hallway. Right?"

We nodded at her apparition against the neon light.

"I'm only here for a couple of days this time. They put me in that room."

She raised her thin arm and gestured down the opposing hallway.

"But the last time that I stayed here for two weeks, I was in this room."

She looked around us at the walls, apparently remembering something or reminiscing.

We looked around as well, like two owls, trying to find something unique about the hospital room. We saw the white bleached blanket, the curtain divider, and the white board with the name of the nurse with a smiley face next to it. We looked back at her and smiled as if we wanted to tell her, "Its great what you did with this place!"

She nodded her head after a bit, and said, "Well I should get back."

We nodded back. We felt like the newest migrant tribe, huddling into a commonly used cave, a first stop before we built our own shelter.

She then turned and left the doorway in brown hospital socks with non-slip markings. One of us was also wearing a pair.

From where she had stood, we could see down the hallway. A red light began flashing from the ceiling above a doorway. The nurses ran in single file into the room. They picked up their white clogs and moved fast, thumping to the rhythm of the alarm. Somewhere down there, someone was trying to get out of bed again. We had watched this happen at least five times now. We turned to each other and smiled.

It wasn't us drawing attention. It was someone else, someone with greater needs, someone who wasn't following the rules.

Later we saw the culprit. He was a tall older man who stood up slowly but with determination, abandoning his wheelchair to reach for a trolley of hospital lunch trays. His lean body and arms spread like those of a modern dancer. A younger female relative stood behind the wheelchair, admonishing him loudly, "No, you have plenty of forks and knives at home. These belong to the hospital! You can't take them! They stay here! Okay, you can take some napkins, but not the hospital forks. You've got to have plenty at home!"

Then he disappeared behind the wall of pink round bodies, Haitian care attendants in scrubs. When they separated, he was back in the wheelchair, the dancer turned in the opposite direction, now being whisked down the hallway, away from us. The performance was over.

Upon discharge, we double-checked that we were not leaving anything behind. The nurse gave us a white plastic bag with the name of the hospital printed in bright colors on the outside, like the type one gets at a fancy department store. She said it contained some things we needed for discharge. We added the cream, mouthwash, and deodorant that had been brought to the room during our stay, as if we had been in a hotel. They would be good to bring on our next trip, we thought, even though their generic clinical labels didn't seem too appealing.

When the attendant and the wheelchair arrived, we rolled together down the hallway toward the bank of elevators and a large window that overlooked the city. We moved solemnly toward the light at the end of the hallway, bags and bouquet in hand. We went slow enough to glance into the rooms that we passed. We felt like waving, but didn't. There we saw people, humans lying in beds crowned by raised pillows, monitors, and IV stands. Some looked out to us; others were sleeping, but all were waiting, waiting to leave and join the flow of life down the hallway.

The Woman Astronaut

After they told her she was picked by NASA to be trained for deep-space exploration missions, and possibly reach an asteroid and Mars, the astronaut says she couldn't stand or breathe and then she says, "There were tears." It seems that no amount of starch in her collar or ironing of her suit could keep her ninety-six percent watery body from leaking out. Immediately upon hearing the wonderful news about a mission to the stars, the ever-human woman responded using old neuron pathways that made her legs weak, took her breath away, and made her cry. Three thousand years before, another woman had the same response. She was standing at the entrance of the shaman's shack, and when her little girl rose from her sick bed to greet her, her legs went weak, she felt she couldn't breathe, and she began to cry.

We keep uncovering these responses to shock. They exist like ancient Roman roads that we may build over but rediscover; when we seek to construct more we find them again. Hardened in the earth, old paths pointing north, south, east and west.

And what will we bring to the stars, in our little metal cans? What will the woman astronaut do with her all her humanness? How will the tears flow in space where there is no gravity? It has been said before and needs to be said again; that we can't escape ourselves, that wherever we go, we bring ourselves and a bag of watery guts, brittle bones, and a knotted net of nerves. We are redeemed only by our souls in all that recycled compost of a body.

There are other forces at work. While we may be able to boomerang ourselves around the moon, we can't escape its pull on our watery brains and how the moon's full face fills the emergency rooms with wide-eyed humans talking to shadows.

I'm not sure what the woman astronaut will learn on an asteroid or Mars. Maybe another place for us to put our garbage? Certainly, it won't stop her from going weak at the knees or crying. It won't stop us from killing each other and starving the rest. Maybe when she returns safely we will all do the same. Gasping in our polluted air, we will cry salty tears of joy, dropping to our knees, thanking God that she returned alive. We will rejoice, feeling hope and gratitude.

And maybe if she doesn't return and we watch her die in a ball of fire, a light burst on the pixelated screen, we will cry with our hands over our eyes, our heads bent like children. We will be sorry for having ruined God's Garden of Eden, our only home, and that there is no other. Like the woman astronaut we will say, "I couldn't stand, I couldn't breathe, and then there were tears."

Good Fences

"Six foot stockade fences make good neighbors," or so should read the advertisement at the Home Depot. For Christmas I'm going to give myself the gift in the Anglo-Saxon Christian imperialistic capitalistic tradition: the claiming of ownership over land and boundary against the other, who in my case is an eighty-five-year-old man who approached me like the white man approached the Indians so long ago, smiling in his beard like a wolf with a roll of treaties in his hand. He asked me to take a walk in the woods behind my house—a no man's land; .45 acres to be exact. It belongs to a woman who has paid taxes on the property for forty years, as a keepsake of her childhood memories when her family lived in my house and she played with her siblings and neighbors in the woods. The same woods my own children were told not play in. A neighbor walked up my driveway to tell me that my children would set fires or might encounter bears. These woods were to remain silent now with only the echoes of a past when all the neighborhood kids were white and good.

Now the silent woods are up for sale. As a tour guide through the woods, the old man suddenly demonstrated spry agility as he stepped over the fallen trees to point out with this crooked finger where he had found sixty-year-old metal pins in the ground. We ended the tour in my back yard. On a small tree my neighbor had tied a white plastic bag marking the corner end of my property. Past this point I have placed a shed, a pile of wood, seven Christmas trees, a million leaves and in the spirit of working with nature a genuine compost pile with matching aroma. Thankfully the chicken coop, a previous source of much neighborly debate, is within my property line.

Apparently the purchase of this land has fueled a newfound ambition and *raison d'être* in my neighbor's heart. Although he has no children and won't be able to preserve the woods from his grave, still he insists on fulfilling his last greedy grab at this square plot of land that will transform his property from a rectangle to a thick L shape. Thus, this new geometric figure will encircle me with my neighbor's wary, disapproving and tired eyes.

Thankfully the process of sale and purchase is sure to be slow. Moving property titles from a deceased individual to the living ones takes a season or two.

Days after the tour my newly energized neighbor told me to no longer put the raked fall leaves in the woods past the new imaginary line, as has been my custom. Now the keeper of woods has warned me that the feces of the six occasional chickens I have located near an immense seventy-five-foot pine tree would poison the tree at its roots. Looking up through the bows of the tree I thought to myself, if it were true, it would be a shame. Nevertheless, everything has a weakness and an end.

And so it will be with my neighbor. The rekindled fire of greed and his desire to own and control more land will surely blow out. His outstretched arm and finger pointing to this imaginary land border will also drop. My fence will be six feet tall and I won't hear him or see that he has fallen. I will be absent from the woods and I won't know if he made a last sound. This is how good fences make good neighbors.

Burns

There are different types of burns.

At the stake, eyes pleading up to the heavens.

Those who fall asleep while smoking, they tend to burn themselves and their homes.

Those who roll out from under cars, smearing oil on their dark mechanic's uniform that has their name stitched on a circular patch.

With a cigarette lighter, with the white and hottest part of the flame, or the heated metal horseshoe of the lighter, pushed down onto the skin, cooled by tears of relief.

There are burns from scalding water—those seem to always involve large metal pots with hot handles for holding. The hot water reaching out into space, its silver hand baptizing with pain.

Then there are burns from the vapors of gasoline; those belong to fat balding men standing in their back yards, burning leaves and twigs in a metal drum, or equally to teenage boys making fires in the woods and hiding beer in a hole in the ground.

In those cases, no one seems to have drawn a permit to burn, not that it would help the invisible vapors, the light-yourself-on-fire magic trick, followed by the smell of burnt body hair.

There are the smaller burns, leaving waxy thick lines and circles in the hands and forearms of women and cooks. A hot pan, the spit of oil, the corner of a baking dish.

Burn scars, like medals on a soldier's chest, are testimony to a life in the kitchen, tired, generous, hurried, and unafraid.

Then, there are full body burns, those accidents so horrifying that we only speak about them in degrees and percentages, mummies living in special hospital units, pain as sharp and loud as the contrast between the blood and sterile white bandages.

Oh, yes there are many different types of burns, the element of fire, the sun and star never closing its eye on us.

Lying Man

I met a lying man yesterday. The type that can smile and tell you his wife was doing well, while her body sits putrefying in his car trunk. That type of lying man. He was a contractor, who had promised and promised that he would rip walls down, put up sheetrock, sand floors, put in a bathroom, you know the rest. It would all be done, he said, in one month, then in a month from the first date. Now he was saying that it would all get done in three weeks, just after he returned the call to the inspector.

It wasn't the delay in his work that was so irksome to those of us who had joined our friend whose hopeful signature ran along the bottom of the construction contract. It was the fact that he showed no remorse, took no responsibility, kept on lying about dates, money, and about physical realities that we could all see. He had an answer for everything, the piles of wood, strewn through the once neat home, plumbing pieces rolling about left in corners. It was his enthusiasm to make more promises that was most frightening. His eyes wide open, his face relaxed, I wondered if he had been dropped on his head as a child, so great was his innocent expression. There was no shame. Years ago, I had read something about the stupidity of evil, in reference to the Nazi regime. I remembered this as we sat, and he punched the silence button on his well-worn cell phone, as he smiled not breaking a sweat.

After we met I told my forlorn and homeless friend, "If I were the contractor I would have rather dug the earth with my hands and cut the wood with my teeth than face the disappointment of my fellow human beings. How could he just sit there, shameless, like he hadn't done anything wrong?"

And so I asked myself, and what of the values of honesty, and the ability to have empathy, and the emotions of guilt, shame and remorse. For all the trouble and pain these have given me, they seem to have their place, securely placed in my psyche. Is it not the grease that allows us to work together socially, that keeps us monkeys from eating each other alive? And reality, that worn out contract that we have with each other. Plenty have thrown it out, but some things must harden within the four dimensions we live in and can't be unthought.

I question the understandings I have of my own life. I have reinvented my own reality under different emotional seasons. I know the temptation to lie to myself. It is a lot like eating candy, once you have too much your throat hurts and you yearn for water. I have allowed myself hours of fantasies in which I play out scenes in my head, where I say this, and you say that, then I do this and you do that. But then the scene ends, and I sit with the audience in the dark and remember that it is still daytime outside and it's time to go home where you are packing your things because we just couldn't get along. There will be no denying where your clothes hung—there are empty hangers—and where your shoes were there are only fine bits of gravel.

Could I be the contractor, and smile while I told you that in three weeks I would be happy? My insecurities swept up and brought to the dump, my demands and anger bulldozed into a peaceful gradation away from the house? No, I cannot. I cannot lie to myself or to others. Pain be what it may, I would rather suffer that reality than pretend happiness in another.

Terrorist in Our Midst

There is a terrorist in our midst, or so they say. My friend told me, her round-faced baby smiling his one tooth smile at me. She says, "If you have any information that leads to his capture you will get a quarter of a million dollars. Not bad. It could come in handy." She picks up her son who has begun gnawing on the one rusty part of his stroller.

"Really," I say. "What is he wanted for?" I ask. My own teenage son has already told me, but I like to hear things more than once, and from different people.

"He blew up a building where they test animals, I think," she answers.

"I got to take a look at his picture," I say.

"Me too," she answers, bringing her baby to nurse.

I look away as she slips him under her shirt.

Where could this man be? I wonder. A terrorist, here in our town. Where would he hide? My teenage son says that it makes sense that he is here, because there are a lot of vegans and vegetarians living in the area. People who would support his cause, he thinks. I tell him that would be the last place I would hide, amongst my own. Isn't that a dead giveaway? But I remember that my son is the loyal type. He stays close to the family and likes to be part of the pack. If he were to live a life of crime, it would most certainly be in the mafia, as he is part Italian and has watched every mafia movie made several times over. Presently, he has gotten into wearing full-length grey wool coats with wide collars to his high school. Maybe he has already begun his criminal career. No, I doubt it. I am still driving him around and paying for the coat to be dry-cleaned.

But thinking back to the terrorist in town, I believe he might not be alone. There are, in my humble opinion, a few more terrorists who, while not acting together or with the same purpose, are certainly terrorizing the rest of us. There was that young man, whose eyes were spaced too far apart, who began swearing and swinging at his girlfriend at the bar. A wave of men in the crowd drew up to protect her but the girlfriend jumped in front of her wide-eyed boyfriend and began to defend him. There was a sudden silence at the bar, a moment of group assessment and the men receded and the rumble of talk resumed. Then we all watched as the two walked out of the bar arm in arm, a terrorist team, their violent dance confusing us all, but only for a few minutes.

And there are those who plan and pay for assaults on their former spouses in the court building. If you visit the hallways of probate court, you will see lawyers and clients conferencing awkwardly in corners somewhere between the bathroom door and a display of court forms. They are terrorists too. Men with their hands in their pockets and the veins bulging at the neck, women smiling violently over the handful of documents, proof or ammunition ready to be launched.

Then there is the terrorist who lives in each one of us; a part of us that is sitting on a pile of well-documented injustices. It is waiting and circling a small room in our minds. The terrorist yells, "Just wait, when enough is enough, I am going to blow this place apart!" And sometimes that terrorist does. The love affair is had, the wedding pictures ripped or put in the attic, the house is sold, and a loud silence settles onto everything after the bomb has exploded. Sometimes it takes a great part of a lifetime to put things back together. There is the trauma. Then no matter how many years you have incarcerated that terrorist, there is always the knowledge that it could happen again. After all, terrorists always have a reason for their actions.

I don't want to think too much about that. But I will take a look at the paper to see the face of the new terrorist in town. Just in case I know him. As my friend says, quarter of a million dollars would come in handy right about now.

Ode to the Fisher Cat

Woe to the fisher cat that came in the night to kill half my flock of chickens and the lovely white rooster with his brilliant crest. Better you than my neighbor's neighbor who came over just as proud to tell me he did not want me to have chickens.

"My daughter won't be able to sell our house. This street was the best in town, but now it's gone to hell!" he said, his ever-watching blue eyes scanning the newly made chicken coop. But fisher cat, I want to know: did his words leave you the poison scent you followed to find my warm hens in the night?

We came upon your massacre in the still of the morning. Here and there bodies, so random were the places where they struggled last. Fisher cat, you left puncture wounds in each chicken's neck. I could see the purple holes in puckered white skin, where soft feathers once fit, all tidy in a row. Now the feathers are strewn across our scrappy yard, and I rake them in little heaps, near where we found each cold carcass in the morning frost.

We have buried the dead deep in the woods, closed up the chicken coop and consoled the surviving hens with piles of grain feed and fresh water.

We have talked about the honor of the fox that would have taken at least one chicken to eat in his den. And how a bear would have passed our sleeping poultry for the ease of the bird feeder next door. We have even asked, where have all the raccoons gone? Their humped backs and masked faces have not been seen in these parts.

But woe to you, fisher cat, for we have not forgiven you, nor have we forgiven my neighbor's neighbor. We had been creatures of habit, tucking ourselves into bed not long after the late spring sunset. But now we are adjusting to new circumstances. We are staying up late and sleeping lightly. We have run the extension cords, put on the lights, and left the window cracked open. We are standing up from our yard work, hands on our hips, looking down the road to give a good suspicious stare at our neighbor's neighbor as he drives by in his Ford truck, because the neighborhood is going to hell.

We are waiting for you to return to the scene of your crime. We are waiting for your weasel self to smell death and come slinking over, and your sharp, cat-like ears to make shadows on the ground. To puncture you with pellet gun-shot is our plan. If you die, we will present you to our neighbors. The men will stand around you, and we will talk about where you appeared, and what time of night, and keep you for a while for show, until it is time to bury you in the woods whence you came.

But fisher cat, better than holding your body by your feet for all to see, we will drive to where Chris the chicken lady lives, and buy four more chickens, layered with all their colored, feathered regalia. Maybe even another rooster. And then we will watch him puff up his feathers and crow into another day, "I am alive, I am alive!!"

Chapter III

On Doing Nothing

Do No Harm

A man with no shirt walks up the street pushing a shopping carriage filled with tin cans. The sun reflects off a piece of metal. It is a can he has drawn close to his face. From my seat in the car and through my windshield, I see him as I wait for the red light to change. I am late. He is sunburnt but he is strolling at a leisurely pace, down a sandy path between the line of cars and the curb. I get the urge to put my car into park and join him. Is he not relaxed, bare-chested, as if he were at a beach? Is he not somewhat like a king, admiring his treasure that is glittering in the sun?

The light turns green, I wait impatiently for my turn. I am thinking, "I hope the light won't change right before I get through the intersection." This is what my mind is filled with, small impulses, thoughts and urges, driving me forward in space. I am dreaming awake, running yet sitting, thinking I won't get through, saying to myself, "I won't be there to get the prize! They will all leave without me! They will be gone when I get there!" It's easy enough to know how to slow myself down. I have told myself, "Stop over-scheduling, give yourself more time." But the eager beaver pops its head out from under the dark pond waters of my mind and nods in agreement, "Sure I can do that! I'll be there. Yes, yes! Sure! Will do!" Then the beaver turns in a swift circle and begins the endless gnawing, "Go do, Go do, Go do."

And what if I joined the man with the shopping cart? I would probably end up trying to help him. I would ruin his leisurely stroll. I couldn't take my shirt off, and I would advise him that he would be safer on the sidewalk. If he didn't have the sense to run away from me, making a wake of rattling cans, he would certainly begin speeding up. I would calculate how much money he could make with each shopping cart of cans, and try to ignite the flame of financial ambition in his eye. Hopefully, he would see me coming and get busy speaking with the invisible entities. Of course, in that case, the beaver in my head and I could join him and the invisible entities—but I can't speak for the beaver, it clearly too busy gnawing.

The light turns red, I got through just in time, and now I am stopped behind another line of cars. Someone up there has stopped for something. I squint and lean to the left, looking to find the cause for the disruption in traffic flow. I don't trust other drivers. Their slow progress never appears to have any just cause. I feel myself straining and remember what the therapist said: "Take a deep breath, in and out. Now relax the shoulders." I let two yards grow between my neighbor, a Toyota, and me, an old Volkswagen. I breathe in and wonder if I am inhaling the dust collected on the dashboard of my car. I need to clean this car. I picture myself fishing the quarters from the change holder for the vacuum machine and getting my fingertips sticky with a metallic sap of spilled coffee.

This car and this mind are truly my prison. I know. I move up two yards and read the bumper sticker on the Toyota; it says, "Do no harm." I know that, too, but I can't help it.

Lagoon

I am living in a lagoon—or is it a small offshoot of a stream, a puddle where scum vibrates on the shiny dark surface between brown rotting leaves. Either place is appropriate for the type of living I am doing. How can you tell that I am living in a lagoon? Well, there are signs: the imprint of the crumpled sheet on my face in the morning and afternoon. I take naps, many naps, when I can. Up for an hour or so, and down again, on my belly or on my side; like a newborn. And when I can't sleep, I drink coffee, tea, and Coke, to keep me awake. And wait for the time when I can stop again, sleep again.

And what about this living? Am I living with a sense of anticipation, yearning, wishing, looking out into the foggy future, trying to discern an image, three points of a face? No, there is no wondering about the future in this type of living. It's quiet and empty of movement. In the stagnant pool there is life. But it is a different type of life.

A woman from Peru told me that people in her country didn't get stressed about work; they knew that they had to work to survive and would work every day without getting depressed. I wondered if that is true. Does a Peruvian woman who wakes up at the crack of dawn to haul water for her kitchen never get depressed? Does she ever stay still under her woolen blankets and close her eyes to shut out the rising sun and wonder what the hell was she doing all this work for? I hope that she does. I know that she must have to grab some coca leaves, fold them into the side of her cheek as she bends through the doorway to leave her home, late again. And what happens on the days she doesn't get up? There must be those days. What does she do? Send her oldest daughter for the local healer? Do smoke and healing chants rise out of her chimney?

And on the other side of the world, I imagine another woman. She sits in front of a computer, the online bank statement reflecting its message into her glassy eyes. Half the house is filled with brown packing boxes. But it is difficult to leave the bedroom with the cathedral ceiling. Especially that spot, the spot that she has been staring at for hours. The backdrop to the stage where she watched him and her, and her and him, tell each other things that severed chambers of their hearts. In the lagoon of her mind she wonders about the new apartment. There she will have a bedroom where she will sleep under a low ceiling, face down into the pillow and remember nothing.

A pool of stagnant water has life; it's actually teeming with life. Invisible to the eye, bacteria is moving, reproducing, and eating its way through the muck. It is an important part of the cycle of nature: decomposition. I like that thought.

I lived in the lagoon when I was supposed to be living in a rushing stream. In college I didn't take any fun elective courses. Courses like watercolor painting or kayaking. I walked outside by the pool and watched through the fogged glass as blond, fit men and women twisted themselves and flipped their kayaks so they disappeared and reappeared, yellow paddles in hand, so buoyant, so confident, so ready to get to the river. They jostled each other in the pool. They remind me now of rubber ducks in a carnival fair, each with their own number printed on the bottom.

"Two dollars for three chances! Pick your lucky rubber ducky! Pick your lucky rubber ducky and win a prize!" the man yelled into the microphone pressed against his mouth. I was never lucky, so I didn't play. I watched while others picked up the winning rubber ducks out of the little stream. I saw the winners point up at the stuffed animal prize they wanted. I couldn't help but smile as the man pocketed singles in his money belt and unhooked the stuffed creatures and handed them down.

"You're the lucky winner! Here you go!" he said. I watched the happy children squeeze the immense stuffed dog or bear so hard I could hear the squeak of the polyurethane filling.

No, I belong to the stagnant pools. Not the lucky ducky streams. My people and I like the mystery of decomposition. We don't kayak. We are not winners. We are sad and stuck. We sleep. That's the type of living I am doing, the type that allows you to see the moss grow. I want it to grow over me in my sleep.

On Darkness

Lying in my bed, I watch down between my toes the TV that sits on the dresser near the end of my bed. I don't believe in having a TV in the bedroom, but if one wants to have a warm human being to sleep with one needs to make some sacrifices. This is one of mine. We are watching the History Channel, which is describing the apocalypse. The screen flickers back and forth between the solemn faces of professors, wearing their casual best and bringing expertise to light, and doomsday images of destroyed cities, natural disasters, and a computer-generated picture of the planet slowly going dark.

I say out loud, "I think I could survive without light."

My bed warmer, a man, says, "Maybe for a while. We have the chickens, but people would get hungry and come and steal them."

I look up to the light fixture above my bed. Its dim yellow glow through the frosted glass dome with its dead flies and June bugs is apparently the only thing that is keeping my neighbors from coming over to attack my chicken coop like a group of angry zombies. I look back at the screen. This is why I don't like the TV in my bedroom.

Now we are brought to visit the dry walls of a Mayan ruin. There we are given the close up on the calendar, its cycles, and its end. Enlightened archeologists have deciphered the hieroglyphics, lifetimes of dedicated study. Meanwhile the calendar marks time; with each rise and set of the sun, we move toward the inevitable end of the dry and rough image carved into stone. Certainly, a Mayan astronomer would look upon the violence of Mexican drug cartels and the militarized US–Mexican border and nod his head, saying to himself, "So I figured it would be." Our world seems fired up, explosive, red-hot and heating. Maybe the cooling darkness after the end is what is needed.

I wriggle further into the warm part of the bed. It is winter now and darkness comes quickly in the afternoon. I fight my desire to sleep with cups of coffee and artificial light. But what if it were not so? What if I stayed home to watch the chickens and the bunny rabbits? What if by nightfall I was making a fire upon which the soup would be heated? The TV screen would face darkly into the room, now a relic from the past. My bed would be my refuge. I would bring my smoke-scented body there early and would get more sleep and sleep deeper. I would dream more. And as I heard an Indian chief say, "Wisdom comes in dreams."

I know I am romanticizing a life that I have never lived. I imagine that making a fire is not the hard part, it's cooking when you are hungry that is difficult. I look over to the man who is now switching through multiple channels. He knows how to survive in the wild because he can hunt and trap.

I ask, "If the apocalypse happened, and there was no electricity, would you care for me and protect me?"

I see his profile in the TV light. "Sure," he says, "but I would need a better gun, the pellet rifle is not going to do it."

I feel my chest cave in. "Of course," I say.

And my thoughts continue, it's always been this way with us, always more, always more violent. No wonder we want an end. We need an end.

I tell him, "Thank you, but I hope the end comes quick."

Dear Bank of America

Dear Bank of America,

I am writing to thank you for your generous loan. The money, as you well know, has been used to purchase a house built in 1952 on a dead-end road. It is a light blue ranch, and is surrounded by a good-sized lawn, and is appropriately set back from my neighbors.

It's a home, where I found I could huddle with my children against the cold world.

As per our agreement, I will be repaying the loan on a monthly basis and in this age of advanced technology, I am able to send you automatic payments in a timely manner. Funds will be transferred from one account to the other and sent electronically to your company several days in advance of the due date.

Invisible hands, in an invisible place, change numbers on a magical screen.

As explained to me by the attorney, your company will draw the interest set for the loan first. Thus, a large portion of the monthly payment over the next twenty years will be used to pay the interest on the loan.

I will have to get up every morning and get dressed and drive to work. Even on a beautiful day, when one should sit and contemplate the wonder of being alive.

Again I am thankful for the financial opportunity your company has provided me to enter into a long-term investment through the purchase of this property. I look forward to working together in a financial partnership.

Mother Earth. I am lying on her bosom for a time, waiting for when she will take me in, and my children, and my children's children. So we scurry, too much like the ants, yet believing we are the creator, until Nature like an irritated nursing mother bear, slaps down her paw and shakes her body. Enough.

And all the king's horses and all the king's men could not put the numbers back together again.

Sincerely,

Customer, Ant

Chapter IV

Mine and Them

Map Quest

"All you have to do is place the little green man on the spot and then you get the street view." My son instructs me how to use a MapQuest program. I am infinitely slow with the computer mouse but I follow his instructions and after the screen melts, we are suddenly there on the main road of Toureille, village of eighty inhabitants that sits at the foot of the Pyrenees in the South of France.

"If you click on the arrows you can shift your view," he says. But I am frozen.

"Mom, just click on the arrow," he repeats with his new baritone voice.

I am elsewhere. This first view is that of a wall near the entrance of the town. I know that wall. It is the wall that surrounded the schoolyard. On the other side there are two tall trees. One day many years ago, I was there below them with other children watching as women in traditional dark dress, aprons and espadrilles, stood on tall ladders picking flowers and leaves from their branches.

"See those trees," I point at the screen, "the flowers get harvested to make tea, linden tea,

I think. You needed to get the mayor's permission because the trees are in the school yard."

"Did you go to that school?" my son asks.

"Yes, just for a short time. Later we were bused to a school in a larger town," I answer. My mind is filled with dawn and the color of the stone steps where we waited for the bus. Nearby someone had hidden a book of pornographic pictures, behind a loose stone in the wall. We had all taken turns borrowing the book, only to make gagging sounds at the contorted naked bodies. Someone actually read the pages, and the story had nothing to do with strange naked bodies. We were surrounded by farm animals—everyone knew how animals procreated, but this was different.

I tried clicking on the little green man and a church appeared at the center.

"This is the plaza," I said. "I used to play the organ in that church."

"Really?" my son asks. "You played the organ in church?"

"Yes, the priest allowed me to practice on the church organ. He only came once a week, so he gave me the keys to the church."

"What type of organ was it?"

"I don't remember," I say. "I just remember I had to give the keys back."

"Why?" he asks.

"Because one day my friend's older sister Elvira came to listen to me practice and she smoked cigarettes. The cleaning lady found ashes and told the priest."

That was Elvira who was sixteen at the time and a poet. I had been glad that she had offered to accompany me as I practiced because the church was always dark even in the middle of the day. You had to walk up the center aisle, right where the caskets of the dead were placed to get to the main light switch and the organ. Elvira wandered around the church where she had been baptized and celebrated her first communion like a tourist, stopping at every station of the cross and colored glass window. Then she sat on the back of the pew and smoked cigarettes while she wrote poetry in a book.

I continue to tell my attentive son, "The woman who cleaned the church was the town gossip, she and her husband managed the public phone and sold eggs, salt and sugar, and cigarettes and matches. They lived there." I point down a street and my finger touches the screen.

"Wow," he says.

I'm clicking on the green man's directional arrows.

We are moving past the center of town, past the main statue, and the fountain where men sat to talk in the afternoon.

"It looks like the water fountain isn't running, but they have kept the bench next to it," I observe.

There is a stain of water on the cement moving across the bottom of the screen. I look closer.

"Look there. Maybe there is still water flowing from the source," I say.

Click, click, I see a house on the right with new terracotta tiles.

"That house right there belongs to a Moroccan family, it took them forever to build it. The father in the family worked his whole life in the vineyards for only one proprietor."

"One what?" my son asks.

"One boss, one land owner," I explain.

I remember villagers saying that the Moroccan's wife was having an affair with his proprietor's son, a thin, bald Frenchman who always seemed to be sitting on a tractor going somewhere. It was hard to visualize him stopping his tractor to visit her while her husband was bent over in a vineyard, but after they began construction of the house with the terrace and arched walls, it was easier to imagine. The Moroccan woman was physically larger than both the Frenchman and her husband; it seemed she could manage them both.

"Now we are facing a view of the road that goes out of the town," I say.

"There, look at that line of trees. Those belong to Madame Peille, that's her garden.

Right there in the middle of the vineyards. Yes, those are her cherry trees."

"Did you eat them?" my son asks. He loves food.

"Yes, I've eaten cherries, peaches, and apricots from her trees."

More precisely, I had stolen fruit from her trees, in late evening hours while she and her husband finished their dessert wine and coffee. A neighbor's tree always held the sweetest fruit. And of course there was the excitement of hearing the warning shot from a rifle and the flushed and stained faces of my friends when we met back up at our meeting place. I don't tell him about that.

I clicked past the vineyard and Madame Peille's garden, down the road.

Click, click, we are passing the cemetery.

"Look, that is where my friend Elvira is buried. It's a circular cemetery on a hill," I say.

"Who?" my son asks.

"Elvira, the one who was smoking in the church. She had a sudden aneurism at the age of 41. It was Christmas Day. They say that so many people came to her funeral that they all couldn't fit in the church and they had to stand outside in the plaza. Her father is also buried there with her. They share the same burial spot. I got to see him before he died though."

I think of Elvira, a poet. They told me she asked her eldest daughter for a glass of water before she collapsed. Her husband, in his shock and desperation, drove her back to her parents' home thinking they could wake her.

My son remains quiet as we move up the road past the cemetery.

"This road takes you to the neighboring town. I've walked the whole way there."

"The whole way?" he asks.

"The whole way," I answer.

Dear Daughter

Dear Daughter,

Yesterday, I got a call at work from the school nurse's office at the middle school. She told me you were sick and had vomited in the school nurse's office. I am your mother and I have and will have first dibs on leaving work to take care of you and your brother.

I drove to the school and found you sitting at the nurse's office, valiantly waiting. Your eyes filled with tears when I kissed you on the head, but you did not cry. I listened to the nurse's explanation of your symptoms.

"Let's go home," I said. "We'll stop and get some ginger ale on the way."

You nodded your head, your pale yet beautiful face showing such relief. I felt like a mom super hero, slinging your heavy backpack onto my shoulder.

I stopped for the ginger ale at the Sam's on the corner. A UPS man held the door for me. He must have seen I was a mother on a mission. I told the clerk what the ginger ale was for. You know I can't go anywhere without sharing my life story. He told me his four-year-old son had also had the stomach flu. We agreed it was going around. I bought a lottery ticket, remembering that I've decided to play the lottery once a week and needing to buy the ticket for the Friday drawing.

I got back into the car, and told you about the ticket and the $99,000,000 I was going to win.

"If you win, you'll give it to charity."

"Not all of it," I said. "I will put some aside for your education, then give about $10,000 each to friends and family. I'd give a lot to charity after I quit one of my jobs, and start traveling."

"I should get an extra ten thousand for having been sick and being the reason you bought the ticket in the first place."

I remember you as a toddler in your high chair. One cookie wasn't enough; you needed two, one for each hand, and breaking the cookie in two pieces provoked ear-splitting screams from you. It was a shocking reaction coming from such a generally accommodating second child.

I reassured you. "You and your brother will have more than enough. Everything that is mine is yours."

You went straight to bed when we got home. You didn't even take off your coat. I sat on the end of your bed and watched you sleep.

When you woke up, you were transformed. You told me about your dreams—there were many, one joining into the other. You're usually not very forthcoming about your inner life, so I listened intently as you recounted your dreams, your brow furrowing and unfurrowing as you unraveled the sequence of events that had occurred in your mind.

Somehow the subject changed and we spoke about the Harry Potter books, and you decided that it was time for me to know what had happened in the seventh and last book. There it was, the tome of a book sitting on the bookshelf across the room. We asked each other to go and get it, and wished that we had those magical wands to lift it off the bookshelf and send it through the air into our hands.

"You get it."

"No! You get it. I'm the sick one."

"But I can't move from here and you're closer and more agile!"

Finally you got up and brought us back the book. Then you fingered through the pages.

"You have beautiful hands," I said.

You stopped and showed me your lifeline. It's long. Our hands are similar. I pointed this out. Then you showed me how the lines on our hands are different. I agreed, but with every line that chose its own unique path, there are others that followed the same roads as mine. I don't know what that will mean. But I reassured you that you had small crosses in your palms, and that meant you were powerful.

Then you went on, explaining chapters, events, and reading your favorite parts of the book, including much of the end. Nothing could ever beat such a reading, not a movie, not the author. Through your eyes, Harry Potter became alive, and the other characters were like old friends that we were catching up on.

You read until you were tired, and your brother came home from school. We decided to take a short nap, and you turned on your side, your back to me, and began playing with things on your bedside table.

The moment was ended. The window of your inner life, which you had opened and leaned out of to talk with me, was now closed. I can see you, moving about inside under the warm light, but you are busy and don't have time for more chitchat with your mother. I am patient though. After all, will I not always be there waiting for you?

Love,

Mom

A Son's Question

My sixteen-year-old son has gotten into a habit of asking me questions right in the middle of what I am doing—like grabbing half-empty paper coffee cups and other garbage out of my car. The latest question went like this: "Mom, if you could visit another time, as you are now, what time would you go back to?" I answered, "Can you get the key to the house out of my purse, my hands are full." As his large hand shuffled around the purse he persisted, "Do you know what I mean? If you could pick, like, your favorite era or time to live in, which one would it be?"

"I don't know, Gabe," I answered, tired and balancing two coffee cups and a plastic water bottle in my hands.

He opened the door. "Come on Mom, think, would you like to live in the '50s, or '60s?"

With the relief of having made it across the kitchen to dump the coffees into the sink, I turned to my insistent son and tried to focus on his question. The image of a woman in a full skirt with an apron leaning against a clean kitchen counter and a cigarette between her fingers came to mind. I thought, "Why would

I want to visit the '50s?" A 1950s version of me would most definitely be swinging between Valium-filled afternoons and obsessive cleaning fits. No, I thought, I would go back to a simpler time—how about the turn of the century? Then I thought of a female ancestor who died of an abscess in a molar. She was in her early 20s; so much for enjoying the afternoon teas on the veranda and gossiping with her elegant women friends. Having inherited soft tooth enamel, I would surely follow her painful fate.

My son began to get impatient and leaned against the fridge as I stared blankly into the middle of the kitchen.

I told him, "I can't think, Gabe. I mean, every era has had good things and bad things happen, like wars, illness, I'm not sure I would want to live in any."

"I know, I know about that!" he interrupted, "but just pick one time, forget about the bad things—which time would you like to live in?"

I was amazed at how his youthful mind could sweep out decades of war, poverty, and human tragedy.

"Ok I will try again to pick!" I said. "But you can't just forget about all those things," I added for good measure.

I put the paper coffee cups in the recycling bin that was about to overflow.

"You've got to empty the recycling," I said, buying myself some time.

"I know," he answered, "but you haven't picked a time."

"Ok, how about the '90s. You were born, Clinton was in office, I don't remember any major wars, medicine was advancing. I liked those years."

"No, Mom, you can't relive a time you experienced in your lifetime, I'm talking about another era, something you didn't experience."

"Ok," I said, "well, then I'll pick the '60s. I was born at the end of the decade but I didn't experience it."

"Now why?" he said, rocking on the balls of his feet a little.

"Why what?"

"What would like you to experience in the '60s"?

"Well, there was the Vietnam War, and thousands of people died."

He interrupted again, "No, Mom, what would you like to enjoy? Like the music, the clothing style or something like that?"

"Yes, the music," I said quietly.

"Who would you like to have seen?"

"I don't know," I said, but in my mind there was a brownish cover of a Beatles album emerging. Those young round faces gave me comfort.

"What about the Rolling Stones, Led Zeppelin?" he urged.

"Sure. That would have been fun." I pictured myself in the front row, standing enraptured with the Rock Gods in front of me, reed thin with long hair and tight bell bottom jeans.

I was smiling now. "That would have been an amazing concert," I added.

Gabriel smiled at me. He was satisfied. He turned, heaving his backpack further onto his shoulder, and walked into his room and said, "Me too Mom, I picked the '60s." Then he closed his door.

Locusts in the Sun

I drive up to a field where a group of adolescent blond girls, sitting in the shade of a tree by an athletic field, are waiting for their soccer camp counselor to arrive. I walk up to them and speak to their bowed heads. I tell them my daughter is bringing a friend today to their camp. I tell them she will be with them for a couple of hours and won't join their soccer practice but could they make sure she keeps hydrated and doesn't look faint on this, the hottest day of the summer. Their blue eyes, lighter than the sky, show no emotion; like silent locusts they go back to their work, slowly tying their soccer cleats. I turn to my daughter and her friend. They are standing on the other side of the car, hiding from my public introductions. My daughter's friend says quietly, "This is awkward."

But she must be used to awkward, because she moves her slender body to a safe distance from the team and begins to check her cell phone. Her hair is darker under the blazing son and her skin has become deeper chocolate. My daughter stands somewhere on the grass between her friend and the group. Her back to me, she dares not look at her source of awkwardness.

When the soccer camp counselor arrives, I repeat my request. He nods and assures me that they will keep an eye on the girl and, in fact, the entire group will be given extra water breaks because of the heat. I look at the girls, their blond hair in identical ponytails, and want to yell out, "See, it is right that we care and have interest in one another. I'm not so strange." But they don't see me. I have become invisible in the hot haze of the parking lot.

My daughter and I will talk later. I will tell her that I can't imagine that in any Latin or Southern European culture, a group of young women would stare at me—a mother and adult—and not respond. She defends her soccer mates saying, "They probably didn't understand what you were saying." I have to agree with her. I don't speak insect language after all.

"But therein lies the problem!" I add. My daughter reaches over and turns up the volume on the car radio—it's her favorite song. She asks, "Can I just listen to this first?"

I nod my head. How can I express to her what is missing? How can she know that in 6th grade, I would exchange kisses on the cheek of each and every one of my classmates every morning—it was in France, that's just what one did. How can she understand, that it is through my uncle's quick wit and charm and the friendship he developed with everyone, from the blind seller of lottery tickets to the bank teller of the most exclusive bank, that we were able to enjoy vacations in Colombia without being robbed or bothered.

She does not know what it's like to be welcomed by the warm arms of young women who have only known second-hand clothes and earth under their feet. Women who have worked since they could walk and yet whose generosity and curiosity know no bounds.

I tell her that social skills, mutual support and empathy, are the grease that keeps things running in other cultures. Here you don't need to work together to survive or get ahead. You can choose to participate, help others, consider others, but you don't *need* too. That is what privilege is, I tell her, the ability to choose if or whether you want to engage with someone who is different ~~than~~ from you. She doesn't say anything. My words are drying instantly in the hot air of the car.

The next morning, I wake up to the radio clock. A Republican Senator is saying that the earned income credit allotted to low-income people remains a thorn for his party; he says he doesn't believe that the federal government should give money to those who don't earn money or pay taxes. The blank stares of the teenage girls come to my mind again. It's a very hot day and it feels like love is drying up.

Mafia

We spend an hour or so, we together, you leaning close to my shoulder as I read your high school research paper on the Sicilian Mafia in the 20th century. My century. We read together about torture, coercion, hierarchy, the boss, the capo, the soldier and money, always the money. "You write well," I say. I'm proud you got something from your mother, I who have often wondered how my womb could follow such clear instructions, so as to make you a perfect miniature version of your father. It's no wonder you are happiest in his world of creative men, sharing dreams and making music. I sit outside in the car waiting to pick you up, pressing the send button on my cell phone, calling for you to come out, so I can drive you back to our home and send you to bed on time.

You hate to disappoint me. And you don't. You just wince, and raise your shoulders ever so slightly, wishing to cover your ears, when I begin to tell you about the world. It's the world that I have protected you from, but that I want you to see and understand. You, at the age of 16, learn about the Sicilian Mafia. I, at a similar age, learned of the CIA and their training camps where Central American contras and paramilitaries were educated on how to torture, maim and kill people—innocent people, farmers, entire villages, women, old men and children. I remember my father lecturing over dinner about the evils of the United States government and its foreign policy—but this was my birthplace, where I needed to belong. I winced and raised my shoulders too. And all I wanted to do was be with my friends, hang out at each other's houses after school and eat in the comfort of our suburban shell. Dictators in Central and Latin America, American companies, revolutionaries and socialists, and the dead they scattered on the dark ground were nightmarish images I didn't want to know about.

Some things change, but mostly they stay the same. You of the 21st century were in kindergarten when I sheltered you from the images of those two smoking towers. But you kept asking why the planes had hit the towers. You were still of the age where you were making Lego towers of your own just to smash them down. Since then you have lived with the news of war, playing like Muzak from a radio always in the background. Violence persists. Another bombing in an Iraq marketplace, how many died this time? The seeping fear that runs along the spine as we watched one student killing other students, and everyone running, ducking from a cafeteria. Still it persists, the bodies lined up lying by a wall, twenty more immigrants with sneakers and sweatshirts on. They were all ready for the trip north.

My son, what world have I brought you into? How do I hold the candle of hope for you to see? How will you swim in these currents of violence? The Sicilian Mafia makes sense, the rules and the structure. Outlined, just like your high school research paper. But how do we live making war to keep the peace? How to explain to you why people will leave their homes, filled with the smell of warm corn tortillas and beans, to walk through a desert in hopes of finding work, when you have never had to wait for your turn to eat or carried wood on your young back. I have made sure that you have always had shoes on your feet. And so, now as adulthood is on your horizon, I ask you to use words, your research skills, to learn, to tell. Will you one day tell us about the life of one of those people? One whose body flashed in front of our eyes only for a second on the TV screen? Tell me who that person is, where that person came from. How did that person move in their home? What hands caressed his or her infant body, before they knew of death?

Smell of Basement

"I love that smell… it's that smell of basement," my daughter says. She is dangling off one crutch that she has found, while I am bent over sorting the clothes to put in the laundry.

"Me too," I say.

"I think you got that from me." I hand her the clean bathing suit.

She hops away pretending to have one injured leg.

"Sara," she yells up the stairs, "I found it, and let's go!"

She drops the crutch somewhere near its twin and runs up the stairs with her creamy-colored legs taking two steps at a time.

I yell out of habit, "Don't leave your room a mess!" but my mind is elsewhere, visiting another basement, the one at 41 Allerton Street, my grandfather's woodworking shop. The door to the basement was always open, around the corner from the kitchen. It opened onto a dark curving set of stairs that invited you, like an opening of a shell, to the inner world, down into an earthy darkness. Even the searing sound of my grandfather's table saw and the new white piles of sawdust could not temper the smell of warm, moist darkness that the basement held. I often stopped right there, where the stairway turned on that largest of triangle steps, to breath it in, that smell.

In my life I have found versions of the same smell in cathedrals, underground subway stations and wineries. But never strong enough to bring back anything but yearning for the authentic smell. But how to bring back my grandfather, the alchemist of that scent, from his ashes settled in the silt of the Connecticut River?

As his oldest grandchild I was given partial reign in the outskirts of this work arena. I could have a hammer, scrap wood and nails. Quickly bored by these, having hardly enough strength to follow the instructions on how to hammer properly, I ended up playing with the sawdust and little rectangles of wood that had fallen off the saw table. My grandfather was organized, but not so organized that he didn't have to search for things. A philosopher by nature and profession, he could rarely answer any question or request directly. He thought about it, and then would go hunting for the answer. I would follow, watching him peering through his glasses over cardboard boxes dirtied with oiled fingerprints on his metallic shelves, looking for the right screw.

After he died the woodworking shop was ransacked by younger men who borrowed and took tools. I allowed myself time to linger in the basement and visit those corners that I had never seen out of fear that I would be bludgeoned by a flying piece of wood off the table saw, or that I might catch a piece of flying metal in my eye from the metal drill. It was then that I found a shelf with nothing but unfinished cutouts. I also discovered a closet, with a cardboard box full of broken china. My grandfather had put old broken tools on the box and the weight had crushed the heirlooms of another time. I sensed another side to my thoughtful methodical grandfather. He was also a man with plans, ideas, who sensed his limited time, and had put things away in a hurry thinking he would one day get around to fixing them. I looked through the box of broken china dishes, and thought that neither he nor my grandmother would have ever used them. As a young man he had designed coffee tables for small New York apartments that transformed themselves into a dining room table for six. The gold- and green-rimmed china of well-heeled class would not have been placed on such a table.

So it was forgotten. And eventually, so were my grandfather's tables. The patent stolen, my grandfather's tables dispersed, and the house, along with the basement, sold. The only thing left is a memory of that smell. I liked it so much that I passed it on to my daughter. Who stomps along the floor above my head, still hopping on one foot, forgetting that we are so alike.

Mother's Day

Mother's Day is approaching and with it an oldest son's graduation. His blue eyes, now perched on the newly framed body of a young man, look down at me from a new distance. I yell out across the abyss (or kitchen floor) to him. I tell him of the tangled mess that was once orderly expectations for my son. I tell him how he disappointed me with a constant pattern of incompetence. I tell him he lied, omitted and bullshitted. And that now he may be lying. And that maybe he has always lied to me, to himself and to others. I am an angry God, who wants the torrents of water to come in and break down the walls of this pretend house and wash everything out. I want to walk away from my creation, let him scramble about the yard and eat dirt.

And still he stands there, his blue eyes blinking. He was born with his own default button. A way to survive me. He doesn't seek forgiveness or make new promises. He just stands there because he learned not so long ago that speaking would only stoke the fire. He just stands there because he exists. And he exists now just as he did when he looked up at me from within his swollen infant face. I can't undo him.

My mind does another loop. The voices of the ancestral chorus are hard to ignore. "Life is hard!" they cry. "He needs to be prepared!" How do I roar loud enough for him to hear me through the thick padding that has surrounded his adolescent mind? He only sees his love, the flowers in spring, and the smiles of his bucking friends. He sleeps awake, dreaming his future. I yell out worry and alarm, "The sky will fall, the sky will fall!" I trample around the lovely garden I made for my blue-eyed boy.

"If you don't do it, you can't live here with me!"

I say it over and over again, in different ways: "Move out, pack your bags, move in with someone else, I don't care!" His eyes don't budge; there is only the slightest clenching of his teeth, one against the other. He eventually speaks.

"I heard you the first time. You don't need to keep telling me."

But I do. I need to tell myself. The party is over. You have done your job and now it will be his to continue or not. Failure is always there, a looming shadow at the end of a street, the one I ran past, not wanting to turn my head and look. What failure, my own or his? That is where the lines need to be drawn. The cook splits the breast down the middle with a heavy butcher block knife. So I shake the foundation of my life with each swing and blow, saying, "You man-child over there! Separate from me, live your own life!"

Chapter V

What Happens When You Leave Me

Fall Squirrels and Love

It is fall and the squirrels are moving back and forth in the backyard, digging and digging, their instinct to bury triggered by some dark mechanism in their little brains. I find their compulsions so like mine, and yet I, unlike the squirrel who pauses only to smell the air, I watch myself self-consciously, my mind slipping into a groove, going over and over the last days of our time together. Like the pleasure of scratching a healing insect bite, I want to go back and view us. I want to tell you again and again in different words, how you hurt me, and how I love you even now after everything you did. And you, your heart would split open like an overripe fruit, and the sweetness and love you had for me would finally come forward. Then all would be well.

Until I blink in the waning afternoon sun, like the squirrel. The fall world is around me, and none of those images are real. Winter is approaching and you are warm in the arms of another woman.

God, I believe you gave me an awareness of myself in this universe and tied me to this body. But why did you give me love? Would not the sexual drive for reproduction, and empathy and compassion for getting along have been enough? Why love? Was it to drive madness into our species? Or to bring forth from us a force that creates and destroys? For I too have desired my lover's death. At one moment, I would have chosen to cry over his grave rather than to have him jump effortlessly into his truck as he waves goodbye at the new woman in the driveway.

God, why gift us love for it to be twisted by betrayal and jealousy? A woman astronaut who floated in the heavens returned to earth only to track down a woman who had slept with the man she loved. Surely betrayal, jealousy, and revenge are compulsions too. Even from that vantage point, somewhere between the earth and the stars, she couldn't stop her mind from thinking and planning, and planning and thinking. "I'm going to get you when I get home, you wait, I'm going to get you bitch!" And down she came, like a furious Greek god from Mount Olympus to exact her revenge, only to be stopped by state troopers, somewhere in the South.

"That's crazy!" I said to my lover, when I glanced at the article in a supermarket aisle. We were doing our weekly shopping, so cozy in our routine and in our home. But like the squirrel that pauses to smell something in the air and begins digging again, I quickly returned to placing our groceries on the black rolling counter.

How am I to be vigilant? God, this is impossible. Love comes sweetly. Rolling off friendship and understanding, closeness and sharing. You made us receptors of love, like daffodils looking up to receive the warm spring rain. Love can remain, transform, go and return. Acceptance of its essence is our only choice. Still, God, you made love to be like holding water in human hands. We can get a sip but it runs out between our fingers. So we yearn for more. So many of us, having to stare at our lover's back. We peek over their shoulder and see the new love they desire. How we wish they would turn and gaze upon us again. Oh! For you to turn your loving glance again at me! God, I know you watch this ballet, the ebb and flow of desire forming like clouds in the sky, and wait patiently for me to accept; to turn my head, to believe again. But I still envy the squirrel that retires into a tree at dusk, to wait for tomorrow when the sunrise will awaken his bright shiny eyes and he will commence the dance across the yard again.

Repair kit for a broken heart

Repair kit for a broken heart

Instructions:

Bathe and douse oneself with a mixture of holy water, egg white, coco cream, eggshell powder, and white flower petals, while praying to Saint Claire for clarity and vision.

Call all your friends and tell them every detail of the end of your relationship. Listen and follow most of their advice. Repeat to yourself the important phrases, like,

"You deserve better," "You're an amazing person," and "You're really beautiful."

Don't call your mother.

Go out on the weekend. Put on makeup to cover your puffy crying eyes and drink more than you normally would.

Keep busy, very busy.

Keep checking the Internet, Facebook, email, for any news and distraction.

Fill out the personal description on an Internet matching site. Try to laugh while doing this, so you don't feel too pathetic and desperate.

Plenty of people have found the love of their life through the Internet.

Write about your broken heart. Take advantage if you have a lot of creative energy during these times.

Try to get enough sleep; don't drink any caffeine after 5pm or you will have to get up and start writing before you go insane.

If you can afford it, get a massage or two, and pretend that you are a baby being loved and cradled.

Pray to God, and use every mindfulness technique you have ever heard of to quiet the mind.

Smoke a few cigarettes; it won't kill you, and it makes you feel like a badass for a while until you get a little dizzy, but keep up the act.

Don't talk to any men about your broken heart. They can't help you, and when you start talking about it, they look guilty and like they broke another's heart and you will want to punch them in the face.

Don't call the man who broke your heart.

Of course, if you don't follow this advice and call him, don't cry or talk about what happened.

If you couldn't stop yourself, and told him everything you have thought about in the last three weeks, while sobbing, then sent a few desperate text messages after he said he didn't want to talk about it, well, then cry even harder. Ask God why this is happening to you, wonder what is the point of living, and yell into a pillow. At some point one of your friends will call you, or you will have to get up to go to the bathroom. And you will start to feel better or at least different.

Privacy and Security

I live with such a confused mind in this era of too much fast moving information, that I recall only words and half names. They pop out at the surface, words that are somewhat smudged, like "Swanson," or "Snowson... or something Sno? You know, the man who told all and is in a Russian airport, or maybe now somewhere else, somewhere on that side of the planet." We learned that we might be, or may be, or have already been watched. The privacy of our cell phones, our emails, our electronic information can be breached. Initially, with only a popcorn understanding of what this means in my head, I said casually to my mother,

"What do I care? I have nothing to hide, let them check it all!"

They would have to sift between all those sharp texts from my daughter, asking, "R u coming?" and my calls back to her saying, "Remember I can't text and drive or read your texts for that matter! Where are you?"

And what would they find? How would they find out that I have unpatriotic thoughts and that I would gladly agree to divide up this great nation and let all conservative right-wingers impose their family values on each other? And what about terrorist tendencies? I can't deny that I've felt so angry and alienated that I have wished death upon groups of people. My fantasy doesn't go as far as to bomb or rifle down people. No, I stop at wishing that a sinkhole opens and that all the selfish, thoughtless, power-hungry and ignorant individuals who have crossed my path on a particular day fall into it. So yes, they might want to keep an eye on my emails and my cell phone calls, because I do entertain these thoughts, but thankfully on very rare occasions.

Still, there is something to be said for privacy. In my life, the privacy about my boomerang relationships has been paramount. I don't want others to know how he moved his clothes off the hangers and out of the bureau and that when I saw the muddy stain where his work boots used to be, I cried. I want my heartbreak and pain to remain private.

I don't want the National Security ~~Administration~~ AGENCY (NSA) to be discussing my business, like a group of my ex-boyfriend's buddies talking over beers about how we came to be coupled in the first place and how it was inevitable that we would breakup. I imagine staff meetings at the NSA. They review the facts based on my texts and calls, my age, his age, my history, his history, my faults compared to his faults, what happened, what didn't happen, and what may happen.

I can save them the time of guessing and making predictions based on our profiles. It's going to be a turbulent separation if he reconnects with his ex-girlfriend, who clung on like a sneering monkey to his shoulder and whooped and clapped during our arguments. Yes, my texts and calls might trigger a red flag and pop out of the metadata if he goes back with her. They might need to assess the level of risk and then do a check of the potential seismic activity in the area because I am going to be wishing hard for that earthquake that the Northeast is due for.

Love, anger and earthquakes aside, I'm hoping that I keep my reactions within the river of benevolent, quiet murmurings. Big Brother can go about his business and I will go about my own. But I will always wonder when or at what point in the ever moving flow of information going in and out of my life, will I move an 'o' to an 'x'. What will I have said to make the massive computer watching us in the sky raise his eyebrow? Maybe I should begin texting every day, "All we need is love."

Stones and Vengeance

Stones

The stone could have smashed the side of his head, and I swooped to reach it, but I saw the cars behind him, remembered years of missing the spot, my bad aim, and left the stone alone.

"Men get like that when they are sleeping with another woman," she says.

You take the truck; I keep the car and my broken heart.

"Only God can mend your heart. Read the Bible," she says.

There are plenty of stones there.

Vengeance

"Vengeance is a dish that is enjoyed cold and eaten little by little," she giggles, hunched over her desk placed on the wall of the cubicle.

Standing in the doorway, I was reporting on my recent break-up. I told her that he had been unfaithful and that this had been the cherry on the top of the entire mess of a relationship.

"What did you do?" she asked, studying me more carefully.

I rattled off the usual list: moved his things out, called him names and sent him a few nasty texts and wrote to his mother and sister.

I didn't tell her how he had laid on his side of the bed, motionless, sleeping under the light of the moon. And how I wondered how I could love a man who was so cold. I didn't tell her how I had learned that he didn't touch me because he was already touching another woman's body, somewhere in the night, her flashy eyes full of desire.

I didn't need to tell her. She just smiled and nodded her head.

"Men can be sons of bitches," she said.

I shook my head in agreement, pounding gently on the doorframe.

My thoughts went to those angry calls. The heat of my indignation and the pressure of my blood rising from anger could have lifted the roof off my house. But like squalls in the ocean on hot summers days, they came and went, only dangerously tipping the boat for a few minutes. I wanted to light his truck on fire. Throw rocks at his head. I wanted to hunt down the new couple in their bungalow in the woods. But what then?

She smelled the trace of my violent thoughts.

"So the truck is insured under your name?" she asked, looking above at the calendar on the cubicle wall, hands folded on the desk.

"Yes, I insured it under my name so he could save himself some money."

"Ahh, well you must call the insurance company and remove the truck from your policy."

"Yes. I think you're right," I nodded.

"Of course I'm right," she said and smiled again.

"Let me tell you something. When you bend over too much, you show your ass. Don't do that."

I nodded. I saw myself in that mini skirt, my hand grabbing at slippery cloth to keep it from snaking up as I walked up the stairs. They had all seen me put so much effort into loving this man. My attention plastered on him, his every move, his every word. I had worshipped him like a minor Greek god. My tender rear end all there, exposed for everyone to see.

"Just take him off the insurance. That's what I would do," she said, nodding reassuringly. Then she repeated, smiling, "Because vengeance is a dish enjoyed cold and eaten little by little."

Stitches

I have stitches that are coming out of an old wound. The smiling surgeon said, bouncing on the balls of her feet, that she had begun using a new self-absorbing thread and she had noticed that some people continued to reject the material.

She said, "Their bodies just spit out the stitches," patting the reddish scar on my shoulder.

"That's what was probably happening to you, but it doesn't look infected; just put some cream on it and you should be fine."

I am losing parts of memory due to the huge amount I need to remember, so I only grab onto a few words of the conversations. Words such as "spitting out" and "stitches." But it appears that my body's rejection of foreign yet benevolent bodies, weeks after the healing has occurred, is a metaphor for my life.

I'm spitting out stitches after the healing of time, stitches I thought were firm and secure, or at least already absorbed.

It is leaving me red and sore and mostly in the area of my heart. What did you do, so many years ago? I remember it was May and the trees were full of new leaves, so at night they made huge shadows under the streetlights. A week before, I had offered up my young body to you in a stranger's bed. I loved you. We walked together at dawn and I laughed because I was wearing white shoes on the night I lost my virginity. And now, a week later, you were walking away from me in the shadows after telling me you had hooked up with an old girlfriend. My pain was such that I bent over and couldn't stand.

That year more tears and more blood would be shed for the betrayal of another tall lanky blue-eyed boy. I thought being married and having two babies would seal up those wounds for good. And they did for a time. But I'm one of those people who "spit out" the stitches. Suddenly now, so many years later, I am the young woman who is crouching down under the shadow of a tree, crying to herself.

The surgeons say once the stitches come out on their own, the wound should heal up. I hope the same goes for the other wounds. How will they heal? Will the young woman stand up, wipe her tears and move towards the light, her hands sewing the slit by her heart with her own needle and thread?

Woman Hug

Joanna, Claire, Martina, I don't know your name, but you came up to me in the midst of a baby shower and put your soft warm arm around my back and held my shoulder.

You brought me back into the human circle.

How did you know that I was feeling so alone? Standing tall in my high heels.

How did you sense my hurt heart? Only a week ago my love had told me no more.

Only a woman can heal another woman.

Not your mother, because she can't help but tell you, "I told you so." Because she did, she has been worried about you since you slipped from her womb.

No, you need another woman, someone who doesn't care what you are hiding under your long sleeves and foundation.

You feel it moving past your skin, into your chest, light connecting with light, the breath with breath. The flame reigniting.

Crying in a Tight Leotard

"I am a mess," I text a worried friend.

I tell as many people as I can about the breakup. The words come out rapid-fire from my throat, with more speed with each retelling. I don't pause long enough to hear my acquaintances' perfunctory remarks. Why listen, nothing helps the weight I feel in my heart—not right now, not in the mornings when the damn light of the day creeps into my swollen eyes to awaken the monster of my brain. It immediately tells me: He is not here, he is probably there … or there … and sleeping restfully, free of me, glad of his final decisions.

And yes, time will heal the wounds, and yes, he didn't deserve me, and yes, now I can focus on myself. But what happens when you're sick of yourself, when you allowed yourself to become the thin thumbnail of a moon, or a see-through piece of tissue? With all of my crying and folding and refolding of tissues, I think I could become an expert in origami.

Still there is little of me to dig into and only small edges to grasp at. The rest is vast concrete slabs of memories of a life together. I try to gain footing and I slide back down the wall. You see,

I am good at loving others—started my training like ballerinas and gymnasts at the age of four or five. So who am I, when I am not giving, loving, caring for another? Apparently, a grown woman in a leotard that is too tight wandering around lost in a gym.

Friends say, "You have your family, those wonderful children you raised. There is the house, the hearth that you have tended. Why don't they fill your heart?" The kids are doing fine, thank God, and the house? Well, I've thought of burning it down.

I'm stuck on one idiot, the weight of his hands in my hand and his smile. I've become so tacky. I could live like a crying phantom in the card aisle of a drug store. I read books about ending relationships and identify which stage I am in. I'm always in a stage. Other friends who just went through the same thing nod their heads. "Yup, I did that. Umm… don't worry; that feeling will go away. You'll be all right," they say, opening their arms. "Look at me now!"

And I will. And everything will settle into its rightful place and I will be glad for it. These words will just be the temporary rantings of a mad, grieving woman. The new mantra to repeat: Accept the change, for everything is passing, and everything changes. And still there is a small voice that says I won't. I will be forever changed by this one. Like the ugly dip in the skin of my shoulder where a cyst was removed, I will be forever hurt in a way by this break-up. I will love again and be loved again, and if my therapist has her way, I will learn to love myself more. But what she doesn't know is that part of me won't. I will bite down on my own flesh first. I will need to leave deep teeth marks and even scars so that I can wear the grief of having lost a love. I want to remember this time in the dark tunnel. Yes, I see the light, but when I come out into the open, I want to know that I came through.

Redo

I took him back. Yes, I am one of those women, the ones who after much to-do about the breakup, end up forgiving. Like an eighteenth-century butler I make a deep bow and then with a swing of the arm I welcome my love at the door of our home, saying,

"Please come in, welcomed guest of honor."

All this to favor the king of all kings, that royal organ the heart. It says to me, let us celebrate, let us open the windows, and ring the bells of this cold castle. My chest fills with air again; I can breath again; my love has returned. There is, of course, the miserable mind, who lurks like a rejected royal advisor behind the throne, murmuring doubts to himself. But we ignore him; he is a miser who brought us only angry rantings of the injustice of life and of loneliness.

And what of the virtue of forgiveness? How sweet, rare and delicate its flavor! When you forgive one, forgiveness, like its sister, love, begins to flow and you forgive more and more. Eventually, if you are lucky, you forgive yourself. When all is forgiven you move differently, you are most certainly lighter.

And who can criticize you when you are dol-
ing out forgiveness? Who amongst your friends
and family can tell you, you shouldn't forgive?
None. You are acting on behalf of a higher spir-
ituality; truly you are in God's realm. And after
you have felt forgiveness your eyes see better
and you see what is really there.

So when we sat to talk again, face to face, looking eye to eye, we began to see another path
appear; one that promised a new story and
adventure. We thought about walking down
it together, this time more alert to the dan-
gers—trees with heavy, dried limbs ready to
break, mine and yours—but we promised to be
at the ready, watching out for each other. "The
path may circle us to this same spot!" we worried, as we could not tell where it went past the
bend. Hadn't we already had some trouble with
dead ends and patches of mud? we thought.
You said we could only try and see. I agreed we
should try and be prepared for the worst and
pray for the best.

We live in a society where betrayal is more
pronounced with each launch of the individual's desire and his trajectory away from
the family and community. Gaining power is
the most destructive addiction on this planet.
It leaves in its wake commitments broken and
sex for the sake of sex. I know that you and I are
not immune to it, that desire for power. Even

in our little world, we want to rise in social standing and swim with the strong swimmers. I know why you followed her to her house. It wasn't just her round behind; it was that "I want this for me" urge. "Hell," you thought, "everybody else gets it, why not me?" The rest of the story, has been lived by a thousand lives; the unveiling of the ugly truth, then a period of dismantling of what we had created together, sometimes reasonably and sometimes with flying bricks. Basically, the whole thing, an embarrassment for us both.

But does life give second chances or do we? How strange to insert a "redo" when every minute is so precious. Is it in our cyclical nature? Are we following deep stellar patterns, moving in large circumferences rather than in one directional trajectory? I like to think so. I am swinging my partner, one more time at the end of the contra dance. Happen what may, I have forgiven you and will have always forgiven you as I did myself. This will be my mantle against the rain of regret. I know I walk in a fallible human body and although it holds that perfect spiritual light, my mind and body are fallible. You are also in a fallible body. Still, when I am with you right now I feel alright. What is there not to forgive?

Chapter VI

Belief and Relief:
Thank you God

The God of Mechanical Difficulties

I believe in one God but I also believe in several other smaller gods. There is the God of Mechanical Difficulties that I pray to when my car engine light has turned red and I am rising in my car seat hoping that the engine won't stop and leave me stranded in the road where I will be forced to wave other drivers on past my emergency blinking lights. There is also the Time God I pray to when I am running late to something important such as an airplane flight. This is the God that I call upon as I run through the long halls of the interconnecting airport, reading gate signs out loud, gasping, "Gates 10 through 24 arrow pointing left! Go left! Go left!"

And finally there is the God who rules over parking, which is for unknown reasons represented in female form, better know as the Parking Goddess. Prayers to her are sent up usually when a parking place is needed urgently, as I am late for an appointment because I misplaced my keys and while I wandered about the house looking for them, I noticed the cat needed food, but I had to find scissors to open the huge bag of dry cat food. Cat owners, you can imagine the rest; it involves a broom and dustpan, bits of cat food that will be found weeks later in odd corners of the house. The Parking Goddess is also called upon when I am taking a second turn around the block. I am impatient by nature and I tend to butt heads with reality as it unfolds. So when I join my fellow citizens in a long line of cars, our braking lights turning off and on at the center of the city as we search for the last few parking spaces, I immediately call for intervention from above.

The Parking Goddess and the other smaller gods are quick gods. Their favor is in response to an urgent and present request. "I need your help now, God, please help!" I imagine that they have a tally and that the more time that has passed since my last request, the greater likelihood that the favor will be granted. So I sometimes add to my now prayer, "Please, I haven't asked you in a long time, so can you help me now!" This also allows me to pause ever so briefly and assess if this request is as urgent as it seems, and whether I really want to use up my allotted favors on this one parking space, for instance. I recognize the triviality of my demands and that is why I have devised this hierarchy of Gods, because I couldn't call upon the One God for such man-made or superficial problems.

I pray to the One God for the well being of my soul. I am thankful for knowing you and praise you for all that is my life. When I finally look up from checking my appointment calendar or get out of my car and really take a look around, I am a witness of your majesty. You, God, spread hope in the morning sky like an artist with an infinite brush. I pray to you, God, for other people who are covered under the blanket of grief and whose eyes are veiled by violence and loss. Because I know that just as You are majestic, You are also present in the individual, small and particular. I pray to you, God, to fuel the fire of compassion and understanding in me so that I can be a better person and breathe more deeply. How can I ask you, God, to squeeze into the transmission box of the car I drive and hold in place that metal piece that is broken? No, I'll leave it to the God of Mechanical Difficulties and to the skill of my car mechanic.

Asking an Angel

I heard a man say, "The fact is, there are angels in our world. Angels that God sends us." It seemed strange to hear a grown man, solid in his years, speak of angels as if he were speaking of any other fact. But if that's a fact, so be it. I need an angel.

Angel, I know that you are near, but can you come closer?

Yes

Will you let your soft breath move across the nape of my neck?

Yes

Will you raise your arm and cover me with a blanket of light?

Yes

Will I be protected by that light?

Yes

If a twisted serpent made of sadness, anger and hatred comes towards me will you step on it and cut off its head before it bites me?

Yes

If a shadow of sadness comes upon me, will you illuminate me and dissolve the shadow?

Yes

If natural forces come and send me spinning, will you wrap your arms around me and hold me tight against the wind, rain, sand or fire?

Yes

Will you defend me against all those who think ill of me?

Yes

Will you love me when I have lost love?

Yes

Will you forgive me?

Yes

Angel, can you come closer?

Yes

I Want to Believe

I want to believe in quantum physics, those atoms that spin this way and that, teasing the observer like a girl twirling her dress. I want to believe in magic, too. There is nothing up the magician's sleeve, just the wormholes of space, where rabbits disappear and reappear billions of light years away. I want to believe in Jesus, that he truly, truly healed the sick and dying and that he walked on water. I want to believe that Mary also ascended into heaven, body and all. I want to believe that she conceived by the power of the Holy Spirit, and that she birthed, nursed and raised in those early years, the Son of God. And that for all her mothering and suffering, the gravity switch was turned off temporarily for her and that she floated up on a cloud puff to heaven.

I also want to believe in heaven. I would like to imagine a heaven similar to the one described to me by a woman who died and was resuscitated after seven minutes on the operating table. She had a head-on collision that was caused by another woman who was reaching to keep a birthday cake from sliding off the front passenger seat. I want to believe in what she saw: a bright light and then a grassy knoll where persons wearing white robes with golden-edged sleeves were mingling, talking peacefully, and of course there was that bright light and an incredible feeling of joy.

Here on earth, I want to believe that you can control the timing of your death, just as long as you don't have sudden bleeding or absolute bodily destruction. I heard of a man who lived for two weeks on morphine doses that would have subdued a horse. I heard of another man who had begun the death rattle, but when he got wind that his daughter was drinking again, he pulled himself back from death, and sat up in his bed and began to speak. He remained very much alive until his daughter had pulled out the flasks of liquor from inside the toilet tanks and was going to AA meetings. Assured she was sober, he got back to dying and finished the death rattle with one good last breath. I want to believe that I too will control the timing of those last moments and if not, at least I want to believe that I'll be joining those happy souls on that grassy knoll.

Most of all, I want to believe in love conquering everything. I want to believe in love in all its forms: the passionate, dizzying love that rips people from the moors and robs them of their senses; the compassionate love that lights up the darkness of humanity, the love of nature,

the love for animals, the love for each other,
the kind that makes us reach for the stranger's
hand. I want to believe in self-love, how it
suddenly makes us beam with joy in the spring
sun for no apparent reason.

Miracles

I am waiting for the next miracle to occur. I see you in the four-by-four square on the computer screen. You're at the center of a video taken on a cell phone by a large woman, her religious vigor intonating through the speakers.

"This is the testimony of our sister, Sara. We wanted to show all those people who have been praying for her that yes indeed, God never abandons us, and He is with us always. Sister Sara, give us your testimony."

You pause, your dark eyes pierce through your glasses, and then you begin at the beginning like a good storyteller does. You explain how the illness appeared, the deterioration of your body, and the darkness you faced during the months when you could not eat or move. You say that you have been praying to God because you wanted to recuperate to be with your son and family. And here you are, alive, able to eat, get out of bed and walk. God is answering your prayers, you say, staring straight into the camera.

I lean back in the couch. It's true; God is moving you away from the abyss of death. I feel relief. I won't have to talk about the possibility of your death with your son or your sister. I wouldn't have to look into his face and see the fear or watch tears well up in his eyes. Thank you, God. Not this time. This time a miracle has occurred.

On the same day I watch the video, I see that God has shone his light into other dark places. This time it was in the loving gesture that a friendly neighbor had given to a hurt woman. Arms thrown playfully around her shoulders had lifted from her years of feeling unwanted. She had been the living dead, moving her body around through time, a dark river of negative words running through her mind, occasionally set aflame by anger at the injustice of it all; the light in her soul so dim that she cared not whether she buried herself alive in her own excessive flesh. Then a miracle happened. It began with hellos from the friendly neighbor and then short exchanges about the weather. Finally a chance exchange, the right words, the right touch of an arm on a shoulder, as if shot down into the air by God himself, sent straight into the heart, set her soul aflame again. The only tears now are those of joy and regret for the how long it has taken to feel loved again.

God, you truly work in mysterious ways. I must ask however, do miracles occur even when there is death? I listen to the radio, and a man's voice with an English accent tells of peaceful demonstrators being shot by police in a country far away. One man, he says, ripped open his shirt to show he had no weapons and was shot in the chest. The image is seared into my mind. It is overlaid onto the familiar road of my route to work. A young man in his early twenties, his arms like wings at his side still holding the cloth of his checkered shirt. I see him and slow down at the orange signs of the construction crew working on the road. His pale chest, bowed out and exposed, receives the bullets. I maneuver around the road repair site, where a yellow backhoe is making a hole in the asphalt. The young man collapses; there is blood on the ground. I keep on driving.

God, I ask, how will you touch those hurt and dying in that far away country? What solace will you give the mother of that young man, when she cries over the body of her son, whose tender chest she washed and oiled as a babe. What will become of the policeman, who, following orders, held on tight to his weapon as it pumped out pain into the bodies of the crowd? How will he look onto his own children when he sees them run in circles around the dry yard, arms in flight catching the wind with the tails of their shirts?

The radio announcer is telling another story. But the young man is still there in my mind. God, you have given us the gift of compassion, the amazing ability of one human being to feel for another, to know the interconnectedness of all living things. To know this is to know you, God, to witness your miracles unfolding.

I think of the miracles in my own life, how beautiful my daughter has become. How my son has grown beyond my height, and still gives me a kiss goodbye before he leaves. I pray to you for their protection and that they will also be a witness to miracles in their lives. So I point out to them those moments, like fireflies in a summer night—look there it is, oh, no, there it is—hoping they will catch a glimpse of your magnificent work, hoping they will believe, and know how to speak to you, God, when they move through the nighttime of their lives.

About the Author

Gia Bernini is a mother, writer, social worker, and community organizer living in western Massachusetts. She has dedicated her career to act as a living bridge between Latino and Anglo cultures. As a witness and sometimes outsider to both cultures, she writes from this unique position about human experience, love, being a parent, and faith.